NEW MILLENNIUM

POETRY

AN AUDIO LITERARY EXPERIENCE
Volume 2

LIAM KENNEDY

First published in hardback

ISBN

Contact details. liampkennedy@googlemail.com

August 2020

Simone
my appreciation and thanks
Liam

About the Author

2020

This work was drawn from a larger body of writing which has steadily grown over the last seven years.

That initial poem "A Mid-Summers Day" happened outside of Kassel under an apple tree and captured the moment in a way which startled me. It's simplicity yet vivid authenticity was a true Inspiration to continue. A complete piece of work like "The Forest" simple, unabridged & true appeared across my page after that walk through a Bavarian Forest.

Poetry can be fickle, yet I've been drawn back again and again to this creativity.

In odd moments an idea, word or thought lodges in my imagination, from whence with a little focus, persistence and reflection, the germ of a poem takes on its own life.

Yes, it's like anything we do, give it your mental energy and whatever it is will grow.

Social Media has grown alongside my efforts where I've posted contributions at regular intervals. It's largely thanks to this active and interested community of poetry lovers that I was encouraged to take a step further and publish.

After a childhood in the British colonies of Northern and Southern Rhodesia, I finished my schooling in Cape Town. Later, participated in a war in South West Africa and Angola, then completed my Diploma in Extraction Metallurgy in Johannesburg and spent 1983 working at Vaal Reefs Gold Mine, then the largest in the world as a Metallurgist.

The following two years were spent travelling across the fascinating and foreign subcontinent of India, from Trivandrum in the south to Kathmandu in the Himalaya with a little more than a small rucksack and my enthusiasm.

From these exotic travels, I returned back to the profane world of study. My studies resumed in England with a focus on art and education, philosophy, theatre, literature and languages, graduating in Germany with a Degree in Education three years later.

This beautiful and deeply cultured language and land appealed to like no other. Yes, embedded within a different culture and language my creativity had flourished and grown across the last 35 years.

Prologue

This book of poetry which you hold in your hands is one minuscule chink in an ancient tradition. The first recorded poetry reaches back to Sumaria, 4000 years ago when the Epic of Gilgamesh was recorded for the first time on soft clay tablets with little stick instruments. On through the ages of the Greeks, Romans and the development of the European cultures, poetry was a most highly esteemed skill. The bards and poets shared the state with kings and queens, civilised and uncivilised. The magic of the spoken word has been the carrier of mankind's tradition throughout time and in this long slow process, become hard-wired into the deep subconscious mind of us all. Somewhere in the mind, we are all poets and bards and should the words not come that easily to some, we do recognise their significance when we read the poetry.

The poems written in this book could be freshly spoken to family, friend or lover, for in the speaking of poetry, it is that you truly liberate it. The words like notes of music, each with its connotation, meaning and significance within a line. A musician would play the script of notes to recreate the composition, here your voice is the instrument, your mind the backdrop of context which enables the poem to spring back to the life it so dearly wishes to participate in.

It is a joyous occasion when again, we moderns, with all our electronic devices, share amongst one another the spoken words of poetry. These poems tell about issues, stories and inspirations which spring from our human condition. They are categorised under themes which are pertinent and modern. Enjoy.

Liam December 2018

Acknowledgements

I feel deeply grateful for the understanding and support received from family and close friends during this on going journey of writing. The resonance from the growing community of followers on Face Book and Instagram, have supported my regular poetry posts with constructive comments, thank you.

How grateful I am for those great poets and sages of history which have inspired my own writing over and over again, your words retain their vitality and significance across the ages of time, thank you too.

Contents

- **Childrens Poems 1**
  - A Bear called Tom 3
  - A Child Once Said 5
  - An unborn Child 7
  - Confusion 9
  - My Red Balloon 11
  - The Feathers 13
  - The Footprint 15
  - The Star 17
- **Fun Poems 18**
  - A Dirty Deed 19
  - An Incredibly Ordinary Story 20
  - Confusion Funny 21
  - Smiles 23
  - Who are You? 24
- **Inspirational Poems 25**
  - Let's Live Today 26
  - My Reflections 28

- Leaving 30
- Profound 32
- Seek..34
- Tango 35
- The Captain 36
- The Friend..39
- The Metaphor 41
- Up Octave Life 42
- Vision..44

Love Poems **46**

- A Friend Lover Partner 47
- About Love 48
- Before the Touch 50
- In BEING Love 51
- Carnations 52
- Finding Love..53
- Fly...54
- Goodnight 55
- If it be Love?..56
- In BEING Love 58
- Is this Love? 59
- Lamborghini 61
- Language of a Kiss 62
- Let love be free 64
- Love is not 67
- Love...68
- Our Sighs 70
- The two partners 71
- The power of love..72

- Red once Blue 73
- Returning 75
- Rumi 76
- Tango 78
- The Dove 79
- The Feeling of One 80
- The Heart 82
- The House of Love 83
- The Love 84
- The Meeting 85
- The Power of Love 87
- The Rose 88
- The Seeker 90
- The Touch 91
- The Wine of Love 93
- This Love is done? 94
- This Moment 97
- Together 99
- TOUCHÉ 100
- Touched 102
- Us in Harmony 103
- What is Love? 105
- Where did we go? 106
- You are to me.... 108
- You 110
- Your Red Lips 113

Nature Poems 114

- A New Day 115
- 4 Advent 117

- Atom 118
- Autum.. 120
- Bees 122
- Constellation 124
- Creation 126
- Evening Rest.. 127
- Green Forest.. 129
- Like You Like Me.. 130
- On the Beach 131
- Paradise.. 133
- Poison 134
- Spring 136
- Sun 138
- The Artist.. 139
- Butterfly 140
- The Blossom.. 141
- The Flowers 142
- The Forest 143
- The Orchard.. 145
- The Rainbow 146
- The Rose.. 147
- The Shell.. 148
- The Spring 150
- The Pursues Star shower 151
- This Summer day.. 153
- Today 154
- Tonight.. 155
- White, white the cold white snow 156
- Winters call 158

- **Spiritual Poems** **160**
  - Beyond-fullness 161
  - Challenge 162
  - Dragonfly 164
  - Emerge 166
  - Find Me 167
  - Fly 168
  - God 169
  - Light 170
  - Music 171
  - Peace 172
  - Searching 173
  - Silence 174
  - Tango 175
  - The Metaphor 176
  - The Music 177
  - The Prison 178
  - The Stream 179
  - Who? 180
- **Travel Poems** **181**
  - Croatian night 182
  - Holidays 184
  - Homo Sapien 186
  - Königswinter Germany 188
  - Miles High 189
  - Shitluck Dude 191
  - The Captain 193
  - The Club 195
  - The Journey Revised 199

- The Leaving 200
- The Malvern Hills 202
- The Muse 204
- The Prehistoric Artist 205
- Thoughts on an Ice-cream 208
- Traveller 210
- When will you Return 211
- Who you are!!! 213

Childrens Poems

A Bear called Tom

I've had my bath am ready for bed
My teddy too lies at my head
He's soft he's brown he's tired too
The days been long him me and you
At breakfast time he shares my egg
His bun has jam like mine is red
Then on my tricycle we ride to care
Where children play me with my bear.

His name is Tom, his nose is black
His ear is torn this is a fact
He had a fall high from the swing
Caught a thorn while chasing me
Watched me finger-paint in blue
Moms picture stuck now in the loo.

I got a hug
I got a kiss
I got the love I'll never miss

Which I give you too
My dear bear friend
Now next to me right at the end
Of a long long day of this and that.

Time is now to say our prayer
Hold our hands me and my bear.
Close my eyes the lights now dim
Time for dreams where I'll be with him.
My bear called Tom
My Dad my Mom.

A Child Once Said

A child once said
When going to bed
It's the waving trees
That blow the wind and make the breeze
The splash of water on the shore
From swimming fish and whales and more

From mermaids gentle, who plait their hair
Who sing song sweet in the moonlit air
Of the sailor far on his ship of wood
Of a long lost child on the shore she stood
Of her heart ache when going to bed
Of waiving trees too the wind she said,
„Please blow dad to my bed this night".
To sail with him the silky blue
with mermaid song and whales spume too
Upon my cheek his kiss so light
Then shoot the moon
in a star filled sky

Ships sail filled with our dreamy eye
We will sing and laugh and dance till light
Just you, just I
My daddy and me
The waves
The wind
The stars
The sea.

An unborn Child

Again I take thee by the hand.
We walk in silence, the lonely strand.
Gently ruffles the breeze you sweet.
The ripples they tickle my toes & feet.
Our gaze is captured in the morning hue.
I feel a movement inside you.

Inside you shines a growing name.
A child begins, like the burning flame.
Of love we found on a star lit night.
The moon shone high, the dew was light.
We kissed and red your lips spoke soft,
Of who and where and when and off.
I listened deep, I heard you sing
I saw a star, a shining ring
Of light it flashed across that night.
To light our name
To give the same

To show that heaven unites
Again & again & again.
This universal moment true,
The magic of just me and you.

Confusion

If birds were Bees
Leaves were flees
Flowers grew hours &
Trees bent at their knees.

The old grew younger
Grass would dance
Life's song was sung
With a passing glance

If dry was wet I bet
On drops, that falling up
I'd stop & fill my coffee cup

A bird was heard in Timbuktu,
To sing a Verdi quite absurd!

Up was down & outside in
I strained my brain
I waggled my chin
I ground my teeth
I smile begins

This all confound
Is turning round
A confused muddled mixed up mess

Why?

It's the colour of your red dress,
That puts me, in such distress.....

My Red Balloon

From the edge of the moon
With my silver spoon
I'll scoop heavens honey
Let fly my balloon

Catch fly away meteorites
With a net made of silk
While slowly nipping my hot glass of milk

Those fancy old planets
Dressed up for the night
Play hide me & seek me
With cosmic delight

The party's not over
The fun just begun
Stars wiggle & Squiggle
Wanting also to come

To join, play & tumble
Right out of the sky
Eat candy & popcorn just like you & I

The window frost covered
Alone in my room
Gaze out in the night sky
On the edge of the moon
Where they are all playing
With my red balloon.

The Feathers

As a feather, fell gentle from the wing
Bunched once together feathered, flight it did bring
    Light it now dances on the breeze
Let this please those souls of sad content
Let this ease the load from madness bent
Let this tease the tortured heart so spent

The feather flies, its flight denies
The gravity of the deed
It floats and spins through unseen seas
Of surging current of clear fresh breeze

Let my children the feathers be
Dropped from the wing once family
Caught captured flung
Spun swirled through life
The feather might try with all its might
But flight, grew on the wing

Lets sing, redemptions song
can this song, in text be wrong?
Feathers lost along the flight
Life's journey long, the wing, the right
The wrong, the up the down
Together once we all began
Feathers on a wing, we sing the song
The song life gave us all
All along

Now old I lay my tired head,
Upon those feathers and go to bed.

The Footprint

Its in the setting of my foot print
That my words begin to walk
A journey across wide spaces
Deep inside my thoughts
The story of those places
Of stars of mountains too
Of hummingbirds and crystal balls
of you and me and who
This world of ever never
It's here for all to share
It's here we touch we laugh we cry
We open up the inner eye
To Fly to fly to fly
According to a magic where bonds release the grip
Where things unfold a story told, a whispered word,
    a place of gold
Not only in this hour twixt midnight and the dawn
Outside a storm inside it's warm
A twinkling star

A princess far
A half filled waiting cookie jar
I'm Talking with an angel
who whispers in my ear
„Of seas and ships and sealing wax,
Of cabbages and Kings."
Friends now gather round me
Your time is near at hand
Your journey starts our ways might part
yet never feel alone at heart
It's in the setting of that footprint
Your words will learn to walk
Take you on a journey far
Beyond the storm
The twinkling star
The secret space where
We just are
All one

The Star

Into the forest, a star fell from the night
To find it we ran like the wind through the trees
Branches they grabbed us bramble tore at my sleeves
On the roots we stumbled I tripped and fell
Then lying before us light silvery blue
Your eyes they sparkled then through the dew
You reached out embracing that distant clear light
I caught your glimmer sparkling bright
Then together we gazed into each other's sight
Yes, it was love that we found, that starry night
Which came with a flash
Sent from heaven above
To wrap us in magic to give us the love.

Fun Poems

A Dirty Deed

Of all the dirty deeds I've done
I've done the dirty deed
I've done the dirty deed indeed
I've done the dirty deed

Indeed indeed I've done the deed
The dirty deed I've done
The dirty deed I've done indeed
I've done the dirty dirty deed
Indeed the dirty deed, the dirty deed
The deed the dirty dirty deed
I've done!!!!

An Incredibly Ordinary Story

Sun comes up and pulls the blankets from my bed, on another incredibly ordinary day.
Ordinary plain simple uncomplicated and incredible.
I take a coffee, as we all do, bathing my brain in a caffeined shower of neuronic stimulations. Incredible this simple done, delicious ordinary.
We all fan out across the lives we lead, doing the ordinary.
Me this, you that, they the other.
No questions asked it's just plain ordinary stuff, which is ordinarily incredible.
An ordinary lunch, mabey later an extra ordinary tea, choose your flavors please they are incredible to me.
Day over, another ordinary day, another incredibly ordinary day done.
Incredible this ordinary.
Incredibly
Ordinary.
Day.

Confusion Funny

If birds were Bees
Leaves were flees
Flowers grew hours &
Trees bent at their knees.

The old grew younger
Grass would dance
Life's song was sung
With a passing glance

If dry was wet I bet
On drops, that falling up
I'd stop & fill my coffee cup

A bird was heard in Timbucktoo,
To sing a Verdi quite absurd!

Up was down & outside in
I strained my brain

I waggled my chin
I ground my teeth
I smile begins

This all confound
Is turning round
A confused muddled mixed up mess

Why?

It's the colour of your red dress,
That puts me, in such distress.....

Smiles

When smiles grow flowers
Laughter bears fruit
Dancing and skipping produces the root

When talk and wonder, blossom in spring
Thinking moves gentle like a bird on the wing
Messages click through finger tips

When you, when I, face the book
We greet a memory, we remember a look
We call back that page, that chapter, that took

So long to forget, forgive, forfeit

Now let's grow flowers, fruits and roots
Laugh in spring, fly on the wing
Click like crickets in Face book & sing!

Is it not nice to be happy again?

Who are You?

to be or not to be. Shakespeare
to be is to do.
Sartre
to do is to be.
Nietzsche
do be do be do.
Sinatra

so who are you?

Inspirational Poems

Let's Live Today

Let's live today with tomorrow's deed.
Let's plan,
create the seed, grow the way and need.
Of days yet come in one with the unison.

The thoughts we share.
The we we are,
The I the you
The never who....& where & why.

Let all that melt,
Blow away on a distant breeze.
Let waves crash loud,
The clouds fly high.
I'll hold your hand & touch your eye,
With thought.
The way I see.
The way you feel.
The way we touch.

Could this ever be as much,
As we had hoped for?

In the beginning,
so also shall it be in the end.
Where again we, one day will meet,
On distant shore by distant seas.
On different planets with different needs.
Yet now is here, alive, vibrant & quick.

I & you & we & me.
Are living for today.
Alive tomorrow,
could the way,
we live, laugh & play today?

My Reflections

This reflection is it really me?
Yes my nose that crazy hair
It's in my eyes though
my look of dissociation
I feel the dissatisfaction
the disambiguation is deep.

Am I ever enough?
My belly's soft a little round
No six pack abs like Arni
No chiseled unique physique
I'm simply unspectacular?
Captured in my reflections gaze
A puzzled furrowed brow eyebrow raised

Can I learn to appreciate?
Can I grow to recognize?
I'm lost reflecting thoughts
Not that reflection there, no

Do I dare challenge the stunning
The perfect those magnificent others?
I've been taught to adore
To admire everything but me!

I've learnt to be insignificant
To tow the line to buy to be beautiful
Is it ever enough?
Am I never enough?

I glance I glare into this void
I grab my stare screaming
"Never, Ever!" will I capitulate to mediocrity again
I've been lost
I've just found
Me in enough
I'm enough for me
I'm enough to be happy
I'm enough to be true
I'm enough to feel uniquely
Meaningfully me.

Leaving

Leaving, we take what we have and go
Leave behind what we do know.
Depart, leave without the one.
Alone again my steps drag heavy from fun,
The share & care & lovingly.. begun.

leaving, I have only me with bags galore
leave find that together is so much more
depart, from us, the fullness so complete...
alone again the fleeting feel now obsolete,
the talk & laugh & completely.. alone

leaving, leaves me quite in the now, still
leave me naked stripped of feeling how
two companions captured in the now of love
depart, to start the day alone again
the touch & feel & fullfillingly.. pain

wind strokes, me, your cheek too
sun warms me, your skins feels its touch,
who holds the softness, you, I miss so much
thoughts brush the smile oft on your lips
my smile the memory of the kiss
leaving, we leave.. The bliss

Profound

Quietly quietly
thump thump thump
It beats this way
It beats this day
It beats & whispers
Words so soft, so sensitive, so oft ..... profound.

To hear to listen to understand
To know those secrets my heart has found.
I think, I write, I philosophy, I try.
With knots, the puzzles, life brings me by.
To answer full clear logic Mind,
Find complex intricate woven fine.
Thought this ought to satisfy...

Yet naught naught naught
riddles call, questions fall...
the answers,
the all, still leave me dry.

To cry, my heart not heard, the deep felt word has gone
unheard.
Let thought define my heat beat strong.
Let my mind search, deep the feelings on.
Let wisdoms word through feelings find.
Answers, wrapped in rhythmic pulse.
Give my mind its life's beat too.

The world the riddles in complex state,
Reveal with my thought felt feeling found.

Profound profound profound

Seek

Words

Liken up this day.
A simple
An easy way.
A word
A rhyme
A song
A laugh
A chuckle
A sigh

Words with wisdom
Words to fly
Words fill my soul
I smile now & know not why.

Tango

When love dances
It's in the spin, in the twist
Moments in movement
Glances caught between crescendo and cantata
Magic encapsulated we
My between
Your pirouette
Our tango.
Its expunge and dynamic
Liquid love drips from this passion, this flow
We have become intrinsic instrumental cords
Strung between love
Harmony and more
Resonant melt
Intimacy stamps the fragrance of eternity to this day.
Perfume the way love moves
To Tango.

The Captain

Upon the bridge he took his stand
The captains look a journey planned
To distant star, it's light still dim
Blazing gold the radiant rim
Of a setting sun,
against a rising tide.
Moon was full the seagull cried
The urchin curled within its shell
A shooting star,
to the ringing bell.

Horizon cut the dark in two!

In ocean deep
We are the few to leave....
the wave,
the wet,
the blue.

Fly, through the heavens on a starry night
Sails filled with moon milky light,
On sparkling spume
The firmament we'll trawl
Constellations be the ports of call
Pieces, Sagittarius, Andromeda too
To visit you wonder, the question who?

Let it be spoken
Let it be said
Those lonely souls, while you sleep in bed.
Received us well,
With both laughter & joy.
We traded our memories, dreams, thoughts and ideas.
We threw over board the worry and fears.
To sunsets new rising,
A waking new day.
I'd passage the cosmos
I'd found a new way,
Of grabbing the moment,
Of touching the pulse
Of living the fullest
Of being my most.

Now waking so slowly
I'll take all that I have
The dreams on my shoulder
Is treasure I've had

Your far distant calling echoes deep in my ear
To find you my friend
The star distant I hear.

The Friend

Twixt the gold of autumn,
Its silver grey, which slowly spreads,
As years go by, across my head.
It's you, who in words in thoughts in manifold deeds unsaid.

Have filled my life & more
Have touched the deep strong core
The meaning of me, of my being more
This treasure rich now fills,
The chest wherein contained my beating heart doth lie.
The wet tear strokes with gentle streak
My memory warm, against your cheek.

Now shines and takes us spinning across the floor.
The dance the tango erotic movement more
We've shared the stage called life.
We've shared applause & moments lonely lost in strife
And through it all, from waking kiss till late now in the fall
Of day, of season, of this magic moment captured call.

We have sung in tune harmonic resonating we
So friend, whose hands mine once warmed,
On cold cold nights.
Departed swift this morning into light
Left warmth, yet I'll hold on tight
In my still beating heart,
The love.
To carry you, across your long and distant night.

The Metaphor

Find your metaphor and fill it with dance and glow
For in the orchard of your mind golden apples grow

Harvest this poetry
Rich sweet and song
Like treasured pearls
To right the wrong
To inspire the desire to move beyond

Mediocrity

Speak out with those throttled voices from inside.
Crack your silence with the truth, arise
Move to your metaphor
Dancing free in space
Fill this life with love and feel the grace.

Up Octave Life

This today is a melody
To whistle and sing
The music I hear like laughter it rings
In the morning when waking
To sparkle my eye
Reach over and touch you
With wonder and why?

With happy and smile
With music and song
It's the new days beginning
To share to belong

To together
To this moment
To here now at one
Let's up octave our living
Let's lift up the song
Let's fill it with sharing
Let's do right not the wrong

The music flows in the beat of my heart
Melody harmony rhythm they start
Accompany song as it soars the sky
For all to hear, for all to try
Join this chorus.
Live the life
Love the deed
Plant the seed
Share the smile
Give and share
Hold a hand
Be aware the day is here and now
Tomorrow for some
Sad will be gone
Forever.

Vision

A vision in not simply an image or imagination
An idea or a vaguely translucent thought
Caught in future present
A vision is sight, light, a telescopic worm hole across time
My thoughts key that lock
Swinging back the gate of blinding
Opening the door of intuition to allow sight
Futures horn of plenty let's glimpse the right

Now, here in this instant of wakefulness
We could project life's vision behind that door
Into today
Into the way we work we play
We create it all, deep driven by the vision of the future
By the vision of the All

Give me trumpets of truth
Give me the fire of desire
Enough time wasted waiting in your game

Let's move the mountain
Heave the oceans deep
Take this step across the shore of daily sleep
Be the vision of a life fulfilled
Be in tune with my greatest me
The World.

Love Poems

A Friend Lover Partner

A friend
Is the one who knows the melody of my heart
& plays it
In moments lost to loneliness.

A lover
Is the one with which the insatiable tenderness of passion
Over whelms me
Even then when far apart.

The soul partner
Together we weave the carpet of life
Laughing as the magic
Let's us fly to the stars.

About Love

"Love is more than just an emotion, it's your very
existence." Rumi
We name love as an emotion
We label love with our heart beat
We feel love through the pores of our touch
Still love is truely more
Love goes deeper
Love goes higher
Love goes further
Love knows all
For love is our very existence
Uniting the polarities
Creating the bonds
Healing the wounds
Of this world and that
Filling our being from the inside, speak out
"I love you."
As an embrace, to include all
As a recognition, of all to come

As a sharing of self to selfless
Together we gaze in love, a moment longer
Dissolve in the light
Shiny, bright and true
To re-emerge purged of the shadows
Eyes ablaze with hope.
Hearts aflame with passion
Minds tuned to the universe

Before the Touch

Before the touch.
Before her hands intertwine with mine.
Before we greet, eyes
Moist with the dew of dawn.

Appreciate the subtlety.

Enjoy the knowing that you're also being absorbed.
Soaked into fabric of her mind.

What ever soul might be,
be it this.

A magical, invisible yet intangible touch.
It's pungency lingers like red roses.
Carrying my heart out of my body.
I'm flooded with words,
Awed in standing silence.
Quivering our lips smile & we meet.
The moment beautiful.

In BEING Love

Be extravagant with Love
Be giving
Be vulnerable
Be beyond
Be seen
Be heard
Be lieve in Love
Be love
Loved

Carnations

You Love, are complete
With the breath which whispers from my soul
The radiance which colours my sight
The perfume of carnations which overwhelms me
Take this me
Hold this me
Be this me
In all and everything I am
For tomorrow I might not be here
But there, where you come from too.

Finding Love

No, you do not need to search for love
You require no journey no barrier to overcome
For love waits within us
Within the folds of silk you wear to the feast
Hidden gentle between the rhythm of your thoughts
Felt at times riding hard across your heartbeat
Love is here
We seek, although we might rise up
Arms outstretched to the rising dawn
Calling quietly into the face of God
"Take me, free me, be me."
Unbeknown, it's in letting go of this
I become free
I become this love
In me

Fly

To be free
To be unburdened
To be love
Untie your wings
Loosen your feathers
Fly

Goodnight

Nite nite, sweet the night
Cuddled with a pillow where I might
Lie awake to watch just how
In sleep your hair in braids in bronze

Fall across a face so gentle, clear and fine
I'll move to kiss your lips in sleep
Move the strand across your cheek
I'll whisper soft, words felt so deep

As not to disturb that rest
"I love you darling you are my best."
Letting go, falling too
I'll join you now and places go

Where nothing, no one can deny
This thing we share
This life, this love
the wonderment of you and I

If it be Love?

If it be Love, let it free the spirit
Let it heal the clipped feathers
Spread our wings
We take to the sky

If it be Love, let it carry our Soul
Higher in warm thermals of passion
Life's horizon
Growing as we fly

If it be Love, let it touch our body,
Wild drum beat of the heart,
A neap tide surging
Till we cry

If it be Love, let me whisper,
Soft the music, words you can hear,
Red red rose
The beauty in my eye!

If it be Love, let us laugh
Let us sing, let us cry
Together forever
Till the long day is nigh

In BEING Love

Be extravagant with Love
Be giving
Be vulnerable
Be beyond
Be seen
Be heard
Be lieve in Love
Be love
Loved

Is this Love?

Let my love grow like a seed,
Unfolding slowly deep inside of me.
The gentle sprout, the subtle root
My beating heart to find the path.

Through the thicket, thorns
brambles and decay
A light shines forward
Shares the way

Towards the lips
Towards the this
Towards those feelings
So dearly missed

Of something new so deep and strong
Feeling found cannot be wrong.
Such is the magnet of this kiss
Attracts me forwards towards the bliss

Towards the now
Towards the synchronicity
Towards the how.
It just happened.

Lamborghini

I've tried to understand this beating
Heart gyration that plasters
Happiness laugher and joy
Across the landscape of my life
Pulsating contoured confusion
What's happening inside me?
The analysis is intriguingly simple
You, alone drive a Lamborghini though my brain
A bulldozer across my feelings
It's all noise action & red flashing lights when I picture you
Laughter pealing away behind the roar of my heart
Others might call me love sick
You just smile
It's Truly infectious
Infectiously ecstatic
Ecstatically me
In love with you.
Today tonight together

Language of a Kiss

The languages we speak
The many tongues from many colours
May be foreign
May be strange
Maybe incomprehensible
When we really communicate
It's the soul which weaves the magic
These feelings don't lie
They personify the truth
The living being in you is mesmerized
For this recognition is immense, powerful real
Speaks a thousand languages and more
Communicates in energetic waves
We perceive sparking from these eyes
Dancing pirouette with butterflies
The strangest thing is not your colour, language or creed
It's my need

To communicate with my lips
The reality of what's happening
With this one
Kiss

Let love be free

I have tried
Tried again, and again, and again
Tried so Long now
I start feeling the pain
The pain of now knowing that never again

You will ever answer the call
You will respond to the plea
You will come together,
to be with.... Me

Take a new path together
See a world we create
Our place of peace to negotiate
To know you returning, to a warm cup of tea
A home as partners,
with just you & me.

It's been passion
It's been love
It's been friendship & fun
Its been partnerships pleasure
Together we one

Laughter & tickles
Excitement so free
Stories enriching
With just you & me

This grace given gift of soul mates deep in touch
Shared by so few yet
Meaning so much

Where does this leave us my sweet darling ?
I love you, you living far off cross the sea

This love we have lived
For so long now we see
How close, how free, the intensity

I now see you clearly
& set our love free
Can it ever, only have belonged just to me?
But with all those lovers
In this world so bazaar
Who share life's journey and travel afar

Is our journey over
Love lived never to be?

Or is it just starting,
we just have to see?

I'll always be with you ....
.... till eternity.

Love is not

Love is not *only* an emotion
Love is not *only* a feeling
Love is not *only* a verb
Love is not *only* a heart -beat
Love is not *only* an action
Love is not *only* an inspiration

It's is my very existence!

My peace
My home
My quiet
My inspiration
My gratitude
My love
My you

Love

It might be day
It might be night
Or some time in between
Love
You might be wrong
You might be right
Or deliberating
Love
You might be in love
You might be out of love
Or pained with rejection
Love
You might be on the way
You might long have arrived
Or have not yet decided
Love

For this love binds all, heals all, feels all, is all we are and
could be
Love

Our Sighs

My lover met me
The wine red upon her lips
The ruby lockets lightly in her fingers
She gazed into my eyes
Which became like hands
My face became my eyes
So we touched together intimately
Not our bodies but our sighs.

The two partners

A Friend;
Is the One who knows the melody of my heart.
Playing this memory, in my moments of loneliness.

A Lover;
is the one with which the insatiable tenderness of passion,
Over whelms, even then, when continents us part.

The power of love

I shall love thee strong,
Words great masters wrote,
they may be wrong.
Let Mine invoke,
Chase that hasty hand of time,
Twith ALL is smote.

The mountain crumbles,
Oceans heave the sandy break.
Sky asunder torn could not create ....

Yet, Still in quiet moments of reflect,
It's you who are the apple of my eyes respect.
My life's moments pass away,
The power of love though here to stay.
Twixt Eternity & Infinity
To share with you,
yet one more day.

Red once Blue

I fell in love the other day
I don't know why
I'm not quite sure or what to say
We chatted as it happens all a while
We laughed smiled
The simple act
The fact of having
Recognized that underlying
Our conversations flow Between our eyes
Beneath a glance or two
A knot of excitement pulsed with you
A bright brilliant ribbon of light
Swirled freely around my heart
Magnificence cast it's spell
In me I surrendered to the bewilderment of you
I observed myself keenly
I wonder at how this happens
I'm thrilled with the wild child in me.

Once Red now turns to Blue

What is this vibrance felt in me, flows from you?
Is this how love happens?
Afar out there beyond
You are now alive in me
Beating thudding irregular across my chest
Excitement in a pearl
A home open to the few
Is now yours to touch
Enriching me so much.

Sweet smiles across the night
To Turn in me the living key around around around
Treasure is this place within me found
Shines it's gorgeous light
To dazzle us with beating hearts
Is this right?
Yet could be wrong?

Is this life's song?

It is new
Yes life long I've listened
Waiting for this harmony melody symphony in blue
Now turns to Red in me
To Red in you.

Returning

Should I miss you, but only for one day
Those hours lost, fallen by the way
Each one cold and lonely, for naught to speak
My thoughts though flow, from morning till the peak of dawn
Your beauty, heart and happy
Your smile, glows from deep within
You do this magic in me, find places new to win

So call I to the rising, the warmth of a new day near
To the stars which also leaving
Sing heavenly you to hear
This day new to discover the love I know so well
My partner heart again will start
Rejoicing with this bell.
Rings with your returning
Happiness calls to me
My love my heart my darling
Again, you are with me.

Rumi

“If you want love do not hide from the self.“

Stretch your face to my warming light
These penetrant rays will revive
Rejuvenate, activate inspiration in myself
Not hiding, but striving towards love
I want this exuberance in you too.

The corner dark and dreary, inconspicuous where you hide
Waiting, for love lost whilst not in stride
It’s it’s .... not really me at all in hiding
This self camouflaged in moldy drab
Enough I have of bad
Enough isolation in myself
The sad recognition, so alone in me I’ve had.
Enough

„Love is not what I here will find, Love is that which shines!“

I stretch my face to your love
Mine no longer hidden but free
Free of constraints which prevented self to see
Love is everything and everywhere in me.

"If you want love, do not hide within who you see."

Tango

When love dances
It's in the spin, in the twist
Moments in movement
Glances caught between crescendo and cantata
Magic encapsulated in
My between
Your pirouette
Our tango.
It's expungence and dynamic
Liquid love drips from this passion this flow
We have become intrinsic instrumental cords
Strung between love
Harmony and more
Resonant we melt
Intimate we stamp a fragrance of eternity to this day.
Perfume the way love moves
To Tango.

The Dove

The day upon me here in the grass
Clouds above they slowly pass
The world is green and white and blue
The woman's heart here joins me too
"Red," she said, "is all my world"
She whispers bending to my lips
"A wish", she said, "make my heart green."
Blue above, whiteflies a dove
Carries green, this twig called Love.

The Feeling of One

Could a ray of light be brighter
Than the sparkle in your eye ?
The smile thats full of diamonds
Your hair like gold & rye !

I touched your lips, the softness
sweet music in the air
I felt your skin, the warming
A face, your beauty fair

So each moment is unique
The clock ticks on
The high clouds Sweep

We find a friend I
We feel complete
We touch the sky
We shed a cry
We hear the beat

The Echoes.....reverberate
Our Universe .....pulsate
My Heart... ....generates

The power of joy
The elation, the fun
The laughter & smiling
The Feeling of ONE

The Heart

I’ve learnt love in the light of your affection
Our feelings embrace, lips they kiss
Joy, dances unseen in my breast
All this poetry you create in me

A transmutation with which we
Discover
Uncover
Recover
The heart.

The House of Love

In this house of Love
I am bewildered with your beauty
This structure is made of music
This floor dances to your body
Listen to the words
As you spin within my chest
For that movement becomes the poetry
Unaffected by the rising or setting
For our home dances through the universe
Hand in hand
In love with love.

The Love

Morning beautiful to my lips
I call your loving into the tips
Of Fingers folded hands on knees
Eyes wide shut you are at ease.

The blossoming bud of a rose in bloom
Your perfume, my thought
permeate the room
With morning joy fresh love on high.

Twinkled glance in a blue clear eye
We meet, we see, we know it's real
It's simply this, is what we feel
The Love.

The Meeting

When we meet, I need not be presumptuous.
It's you that I want to discover though.
The nuances of what you say
Whispered, in slow motion
The firm fingers curling into mine seeking warmth
It's in this moment, fleeting toward sunset
We spin threads of togetherness
Whispy fine silk sashes
Flash red from the horizon
To embrace your lips
To embody our relationship

Love, with us in flow
Love, we laugh we know
Love, we are divine
Love, with us will grow

We will be enhanced by that which is Love
Let go of harshness to discover compassion

Receiving reassurances which tingles in our ears
Of all we see, we hear, we feel, we touch,
Only love
Will stretch to eternity
Will resound to Infinity
Will unite this all, this much.
Will bind the bond of this moment
Forever.

The Power of Love

„I shall love thee strong“,
Words great masters spoke
they may be wrong
Let Mine invoke
Chase that hasty hand of time, with ALL is smote

Yet then the Mountains crumble
Oceans heave the sandy break
Sky is torn asunder it could not create

Yet, still in quiet moments of reflect
It's you who are the apple of my eyes respect
My life's moments pass away
The power of my love though here to stay

Twixt, eternity & infinity
Naught but love holds time at bay
To share with you
yet one more happy day

The Rose

If she loves
She lives and touches me
Is it serendipity?
A blossom opens to receive the morning light

The perfumed aura of delight
Breathless from this rose in red
Her sight alone leaves me dizzy
Perfect her figure saturates my head

The rose, the red
The unspoken, the said
The synchronicity of how
This came to be

A magic web of we
A thread you spin
A heart pulse makes the sound
A flower in you is found

The Rose

The Seeker

by Liam
When it's the moon and stars I seek
Let me embrace the night
When I place a rose in your palm
It's not the thorns which distract
It's your deep eyes which hold me
When it's love I seek
The reflection of your smile reminds me
Our hearts are laughing
For yet another day together.

The Touch

First we gently touch
It turns out the thoughts
Your mindfulness is an embrace
My hands run through your space

Where you stand with distinction
Air you fill with beauty
My thoughts caress
Those lips I yearn no less

Your features fascinate me
The curve, the flow of beauty around your cheek
Hips I seek to understand
A cascade in gold tumbles across your brow

The blue in heaven
Sparking from your eye
I know you, not who or why
Yet, you have entered my pulse

Melted into me as if you were always meant too
I know the cherry sweet
Will fill, the still quiet wonder in my gaze
Amazing this moment of recognition

This eternity of who
This infinity of you

The Wine of Love

This wine of love from which we sip
Is to live a timeless memory
For naught else exists other than to discover love
“Nothing is left to do but die,” said I
“Alone knowing my name is life enough”, said love
In speaking with love
It’s life which returns
To the seekers.
In being with love
It’s life which returns
To the the skeptics
“Why bother with time at all?”
“It’s in timelessness we are kissed,
Each with a sip of love,” said I.

This Love is done?

I have tried
Tried again, and again, and again
Tried so Long now
I start feeling the pain
The pain of now knowing that never again

You will ever answer the call
You will respond to the plea
You will come together
to be with.... Me

Take a new path together
See a world we create
Our place of peace to negotiate.
To know you returning, to a warm cup of tea
A home as partners
with just you & me

It's been passion
It's been love
It's been friendship & fun
Its been partnerships pleasure
Together we one

Laughter & tickles
Excitement so free
Stories enriching
With just you & me

This grace given gift of soul mates deep in touch
Shared by so few yet
Meaning so much

Where does this leave us my sweet darling bee?
I love you, you living far off cross the sea

This love we have lived
For so long now we see
How close, how free, the intensity

I now see you clearly
& set our love free
Can it ever, only have belonged just to me?
But with all those lovers
In this world so bazaar
Who share life's journey travel afar

Is our journey over
Love lived never to be?
Or is it just starting
we just have to see?

I'll always be with you till eternity

This Moment

When we meet, I need not be presumptuous
It's you that I want to discover though
The nuances of what you say
Whispered, in slow motion
The firm fingers curling into mine seeking warmth
It's in this moment, fleeting toward sunset
We spin threads of togetherness
Wispy fine silk sashes
Flash red from the horizon
To embrace your lips
To embody our relationship
Love, with us inflow
Love, we laugh we know
Love, we are divine
Love, with us, will grow
We will be enhanced by that which is Love
Let go of harshness to discover compassion
Receiving reassurances which tingle in our ears
Of all we see, we hear, we feel, we touch

Only love
Will stretch to eternity
Will resound to Infinity
Will unite this all, this much.
Will bind the bond of this moment
Forever.

Together

From me to you
a sweet goodnight
Through lonely hours of starry light
Till day it dawns and with new start

You awaken deep within my heart
Dreams we've shared are intertwined
With memories, moments their to find
When touch & talk & laughter free

Illuminate the need to be
Together we share the oneness
Grown fondness, fairness all togetherness
A you
An I
In union we can brave the sky.

TOUCHÉ

In my every cell I find you
Feel you surging through my blood
Throw myself into the wild liquid of your love
Lost now in our after glow of morning
I find memories of who we were
Like wild flowers woven into the golden of your hair
Transformation creates this magic, being in the bliss.
Who care's its the moment captured,
Our first ever loving kiss.

Four wings in silver shining
We are angels brilliant bright
Heavens calling us to table each and every night.
Yours, mine and all who seeking
Fly with us, hand in hand.
This day now draws to slumber
The morning bright your band.

Brings gold, brings stars, brings light and more
The waves they crash and cry and roar
The liquid sea, the love, the moment, me you and it all.
We gently touch caressing call
Touché Cherie

Touched

I speak to you
More often than not
Without words or syllables
It's my silence
Which reverberates when it's you, I see
Not with my eyes
In my mind, it's me
You have become.
Your beauty betrayed my need for harmony
Breathtaking, I gasped
In the moment between a heart beat,
a smile and the thought which set you free again.
Love touched the infinity of who we are
The immensity of what happened to me

Us in Harmony

Loves affirmation transforms us
The lover in you
The beloved in me
Love transcends to Creativity

Evoking a mysterious desire.
Stirs the dragon burns the fire
We touch with heart
We touch with fingertip
We touch with thought

This 'Berührung'
Aught it mean so much?
But I am,
Caught in the meaning
Amazed with the simplicity
Enraptured by its depth
Upgraded on this powerful surge
The transmutation from simple to unification

To this!

Its love
It's you & me
It's more than our synchronicity
Yes us just
In
Harmony

What is Love?

Loves *joy* is the wild laughter we together found.
Loves *magic* is the glue holds together when unbound.
Loves *being* is the silent power within all life.
Loves *integrity* is the truth which holds beyond the strife.
Loves *presence* is the quiet whisper when alone.
Loves *secret* is the truth we share to build a home.
Loves *home* is the heartbeat which creates the ground.
Loves *ground* a fertile place these seeds are found.
Loves *seeds* we share throughout the day.

With everyone in every way

Where did we go?

No, it's not often we lie wrapped in one another
Hearts beating fast & fantastic flashes lighting up our eyes
We breath low slow gulps of reality,
You return, I retrieve my individuality
From out there amongst the planets
We flew high we come back deep
Looking bewildered
The beauty of the moment pulls back like tide across the heaving ocean
Wavelets of love light spring glittering silver
Lighting this halo of momentary magic around your face
My body waits now pearled in beads
My mind though, a float, a-sail on that distant sea
Calls Athena to take us back,
Reunite us in the passion from whence we came
That place is barren now without this love
Without this line of letters
To capture it, warm and gentle with thy hand

It's not often we lie spread eagled
Pinned to life by Cupid's arrows
Crying, not from pain but from joy, from feeling
Overwhelmed that this could go so deep, so far
So excruciatingly
close to nirvana

These are those moments
Moments which define life, as this moves in me
As this moves with you too
We return
Yet we arrive
with something new
To keep close, to keep clear, to keep safe.

You are to me....

Could a ray of light be brighter,
Than the sparkle in your eye ?
The smile thats full of diamonds,
Your hair like gold & rye !

I touched your lips, the softness
sweet music in the air.
I felt your skin, the warming
A face, your beauty fair.

So each moment is unique
The clock ticks on
The high clouds Sweep

We find a friend I
We feel complete
We touch the sky
We shed a cry
We hear the beat

TheEchoes.....reverberate
our Universe .....pulsate
my Heart... ....generates

The power of joy
The elation, the fun
The laughter & smiling
The Feeling of ONE.

You

On that evening, late
After you walked into my room
Fascination grabbed me, your smile too
A joy rang resonating in the key hole
Where I lived
My heart hiding in the cupboard
A closet reserved for tears
The draws, each with crumpled memories
Musty that place!
Rusty the hinges
I had be moving on.

It came again
The vibration, unmistakable strong
Boy!
I breathed deeply, sighing

Glowing, your radiation fixed me to the picture
The wall swayed with my breath
Permeated
I reached out
You grasped my hand
The movement as you slipped into my arms.

I breathed you in, awash in perfume
I beat you off with a hammering chest
I brushed the fluff on your cheek
I whispered in case
Reality was but my fantasy

"Hi"

She drew back
her eyes
Murky crystals
My gaze held the moment which
Touched the me I'd yet grow to become.

"You're beautiful"
She loosened a hand, tugging gently kissed me
Invisible blood dripped from my love wounded lips

Dissolving we both left those lovers
Only a moment
In eternity we soared
Only a second
In infinity we sighed

Smiled laughed and died
Were resurrected to a new born day

"Yes, it is you."
I heard us say.

Your Red Lips

The morning might bring the light
My eyes not quite open to the day
Dance, laughter, ring across my chest
Your patterns, your movements, your art
Your red lips they part.
These, are the words they say:
Letters, join to love across my heart
You take me
You hold me too
You breathe my admiration
Morning, alive the light which moves in you
Joins the dance, the tune is love so true
Turn, spin and fly
In my hand, your gentle helpful sigh.
You found me
I hold you
We write these words profoundly
It's the day, it's love to live and to be found.

Nature Poems

A New Day

When morning breaks
Scattered dew drops catch the light
Reflecting sunbeams, rainbows filled with colours bright
That mighty orb fills the sky so blue
Soft fluffy clouds in white invite
This day to play, create, invigorate a new

Let's take the waiting deed in hand
Rub the sand from dreary shores of sleep
My hand, to turn anew the page
The story book of who
I am, you are, we to want be & go

Awake the dream & live it with life,
with love with all the manna warming morning from above

You might be here, I be there
Our paths do cross, we are aware of how unique
The day of given time

From waking until sleep
Is here to share.
For nothing of its worth we may keep

Till again we fall again

So deep
To realms of endless sleep.

4 Advent

Kertzen brennt. Cookies warm,
Dich im Arm.
Lichter bunt,
Lächeln gesund
Gesang in der Luft
Weihnachts Duft.
Tannen Grün,
Schnee so Weis,
Wir gehen nach Haus.
Zum Weihnachts Schmaus.
Ein
Fröhliche Weihnachten

Atom

Within the atom lies an entire universe
the positivity
the negativity
the electrons
fly in waves
Or orbits of possibilities
Quantum not quantity
Holds sway
This magnificence is in me too
Be it cells, the enzymes
Hormones, blood or muscle
it's profound,
it's deep,
it's within a field of energy
My heart leaps kicking heals with amazement
How our kind has come to be
This unique epiphany
Let's also call it Joy and make me free
Free to fly.

Have you too flown to that place of peace?
That home of all, from which a call
Resonates each and every waking day
It's in the invisible
The atom, cell or sky
We need to look
We need to laugh
We need to coagulate
Around the reality of nothing
To find it
All

Autum

Autumns gold nips chilly at my finger tips,
Pale blue spreads fresh, across an open sky,
A Lark ring sings cheerful echoes passing by
Peaceful captured, moment morning here am I.

The Beech crown sheds its leaf so slow
Golden treasure scattered freely far below
While Chestnut throws in handfuls free, Brown round nuts,
seeking happy children find with glee.

The wild rose reds & mauves now dry,
It's fragrant perfumed memory,
still paint my inner eye.
While rose hip swollen buds await the fearless touch,
From those whom thorns & jelly mean so much.

Fields fresh shawn, grain set free
Harvest past let merry be,
the folk, the farmer, you & me

It's time to take that cup of tea.
Autumns turning chime, the season here to be.

Bees

She crawls brushes twists
Swarms the tulips red mauve throne

Hovers spilling flashes
Blues hues reflections
Across sprouting fields

Stalks screeching green,
Lighting powders stamen fluffing
Seedy yellows

Bzzzzz bzzzzz buzz
Wavering the comb
Wafting the breeze
Sticky gold
Hive

These bees
Float sprinkling
Yellow dust filling
Natures
Needs

Blown miles flung wide
Touches squiggles blossoms begging
Quiver

These bees

Constellation

Walk away, the day dying behind me
Night opens, receiving its cosmic delight
Poured out across heaven
So rich and so deep
Beauty, wonder and awe
Hold me cradled in the dark
The star-shine of silver
Eyes lost in the light
My heartbeat moves with the heavens
Peace prevails at the moment
Carried to sleep this now blankets my sight
For tomorrow will shake me
Rattle, wake me
To new destinations
To new constellations
To new imaginations
I found walking

I found wondering
I found pondering
This magnificent life.

Creation

We came spinning out of nothingness
Leaving behind a trail
Starlight twinkling in the darkness
Dust and nebula create galaxies
Forming stars and planets
All this
While we dance
Hand in hand
Face to face
Back to light that we came from.

Evening Rest

As this day now leaves to lie
Rays once warm they fill the sky
In colours changing to heaven bright
The blues to hues of reds, the white the golden might
Of a day departed and with me too
One more moment of bliss complete
Of touch and love of fleeting happy you

Yes, you an angel dancing high
Dancing clouds you cross my eye
Your horizon lies with me this day
You fill the night with a starry sky

with sparks
with thoughts
with dreams
with intervening flashes we unite

Build a picture, a cosmology
A heaven, a party book of light
Closing now my eyes to sleep
The wonder in my breast I'll keep
Till waking neigh on mornings wing
A new, a day together we'll sing
Good Night.

Green Forest

What is your life about anyway?
Running to be someone
Racing from the quiet and peace
Release that impulse of pain
Demand and gain
Within the green canopy of the forest
A blossom waits your caress
Be blessed without the game
Soul
Your own kingdom to regain.

Like You Like Me

Everything begins
In the invisible
Growth is expansion and inclusion
To fruition then onto decay
Like you
Like me
Within the space of a breath
We came and again return
This is with all and everything true
Like me
Like you
Between energy and gravitation
Dark matter and black holes
The essence
is and always will be true
Like me
Like you

On the Beach

As I lie here weak not strong,
My head rings clear and full with song,
Of deeds and places friends long gone.

The splash of ripple on the beach.
Warm soft sand within my reach.
Sweet high clouds in a cobalt sky.

Floating on this moment free,
Its you who moves in me the how.
Whose reach touches the me the now.

I am in me and you are she.

We communicate our intimacies,
We communicate our intrinsic feelings.
We communicate the idiosyncrasies of togetherness.

Unknown to those other mortals on the beach.
Each captivated in their own exploratory world of now.
I let the ripples relax and cleanse,
Sand washes deep,
This cleans the lens of thoughts, creative and benign.
Its here we meet and share,
The simplicity of Profound.
The exact'ty of the boundless found.

The joy is not being held in the identity of me,
I'm experiencing the freedom of the we.

As I lie here weak not strong,
My head rings clear and firm and strong.
The splash the ripples on the beach,
Soft the sand within my reach.
The warmth that holds and sets me free,
The cobalt blue in the sky I see.

Paradise

The cherry picked and eaten
The day so ripe and blue
Your lips they shine like deep red wine
I laugh and so do you

As wild and sweet the berry
The buzz of bees they sing
In the air your golden hair
Shines with the bell that rings

The fruit the life the loving
The way our journey spins
To that place in paradise
The end where this begins

Poison

Your presence spikes me
Your words too
like the spiders bite noxious poison
Corrupts the spelling
A Blackened web spreads
Pain against which the antihistamine in my mind shrivels
It's killing this
Sweet death we have played
Coagulated the red blood
While breathing I slowly choked
Not lack of air, absence of love
Froze the morning light
Taking my sight to distant barren landscapes
Alone, bones bleached
I stand await
Darkness take me beyond that heavy door of day

Let night come
Away
Away
Away

Spring

It’s the leaves in spring, about to bud
Which swell and greet the coming flood
Of warmth, the surge a puddle of mud
On branch, on twig, on every stem
Chlorophilled life is hidden within
A waiting blossom
A patient leaf
An insect becomes the quiet thief
Will furl it’s wing, take to the sky
The blossom, a bee to the pollen will cry
An ode to glorify this day

Its spring again
It’s life anew
It’s bud, blossom and green leaf too
In this all abundant day

We rejoice we laugh and say
Yes yes yes
The beauty of life is true

Sun

Oh my beloved, when you gaze
Eyes fixed on that warm distant star
What you see is not me
It's beyond that light we recognize
A place brighter, clear more radiant
Let's reach out then
Plucking this fruit, this cosmic apple from heaven
For alone it, will give us the inspiration to love
Strength to transform
That, what we must do
This, what we have become
To be closer, more authentic, more spiritual.

The Artist

There is an artist
There was an artist
There always will be an artist
Which is you!
You, painting life through your existence
Creating the morning with its glory and gold
Moulding from invisible to magnificent
All and everything in awe
This star has raised invisible in the soul
Its shine is beyond sight
Its light is beyond the
Mighty surge of surf
Just infuse the energy
Reach out
Be Come Art

Butterfly

My glimpse was caught as it fluttered by,
A blur of blue in a bright warm sky
It danced, it skipped, it floated high

Carried by air
On the whiff of a dream
To seek a destination green
A flower, a colour, a place unseen

This creature born, is light & free
Reminding us to watch, to see, to feel, the simplicity

All around, with all their might
Our senses move on buttered flight

The butterfly
Is teaching us, to touch with sight
With sound, with taste, with love

The gift our World, from God above

The Blossom

Out beyond the right and the wrong
You will find a field green and sky
Don't wait for tomorrow
Don't even be entangled with yesterday
Meet me
Let the grey of today
Slide from your mind, fly
For its now
In this very moment
That flower blossoms
It's yours, mine too
Forever

The Flowers

A bowl of flowers, on the table stood.
In a pool of sun, the wet colors stood.
Like a watercolour painting which
Timelessly spins.
Radiate, streaming sweet scent and the stems.
Stamen, petals, blossoms woven,
Held a dancing bouquet.
By a crystal bowl now mine she did say.
My mothers gift, from her mothers hand too.
The colours it's carried from me onto you.
From her onto me then out and away.
Fill me with joy, sweet memory this day.
Of the daffodils, chrysanthemums and lilacs too.
Of lilies in blossom of red roses and you.
Days now no longer, but full blossom, sweet scented care.
Of moments like these, when you're no longer there.
Still, beauty shines inward caught in a vase.
The flowers, the memories, the joys and your charms.

The Forest

Let cathedrals come & go
Spires reach higher this I know
Domes spread over, vast clad in stone
Is Divinity tied to man alone?

Walk but in a forest, wet & tall
Black Beech trunks stretch & enthral
Branches arches leafed & firm
Breaking light beams down confirm

An auditorium
vastness cut through with wood.
A coliseum
colossal trunks since time has stood
An amphitheatre
stage the seasons changing mood

Embrace me with insignificance
Wrap me in inconsequence

Stun me towards integration
Enthral me beyond imagination

The wood
The wet forest
The wet fresh leaves
The wet perfumed bark
The wet chummed humus

Drops roll Off the leaf
Clear streaks down caress my cheek
Filigran green consumes the light
Absorbed, I share in all Gods might.

The Orchard

White lilies of the field
Agapanthus, chrysanthemum & pungent carnations from the valley
These kisses fill my basket
The promise, an urge to saturate your air
Then breathe it in with summer
To perfume your senses.
To plant an orchard of cherry blossom in your heart
Then deep in the autumn of life
The sweet red fruit digested
Our bodies nourished and strong
Spit out the pips of our togetherness
Kernels pregnant with spirit
Enriching those fields from which we so freely plucked in youth

The Rainbow

Your way begins over there
On the other side of the sky
The bridge there is a rainbow of love
It connects us to all and everything
Believe not your eyes
It's your heart which needs to step out
Not blinded by light
But intoxicated with color
Singing with the birds
For those wings are yours too, to fly
Those songs are yours too, to recite
As poems of how we have come to be
So alive, so much more, so free.

The Rose

If she loves,
She lives and touches me.
In my sensitivity,
A blossom opens to receive the morning light.
The perfumed aura of delight.
Breathless from a rose in red.
Her sight alone leaves me dizzy.
Perfect her form saturates me.

The rose, the red, the unspoken, the said, the magnificent
vibrant now.

I wonder how this came to be.

A magic web of we.
A thread you spin to me.
A heart pulse makes the sound.
A flower in love is found.

The Shell

Whilst walking forth upon a shelly strand
Squeak fresh grains of salty sand
Crunch & grind, waves surge & pound
I stoop & scoop, a thing profound
I'd found.

An unknown form of sheer delight
This thing unique to me
I question creations geometry
What genius deep in cosmic mind
Did Create this fantasmagorical find?

A Subtle touch of starry light
Spinning far in some galactic night
Weave forming threads, gestalt begins
Evolutionary cosmology
Geometrical congeniality

The spiral form unfolds in loops
Filigran structure convolutes
A galactic form finds growing life
The planet spins
Thousands spawn, new life begins, a thing is born.

Braced between the wet & lee
Feet awash in froth blown sea
This microcosmic miracle lies
The macro cosmic in the sky's

Asleep it's secrets keep me high
I live the question, meaning, why?

The Spring

From the mountain falls the crashing spring
This water growth, all living things
From my soul
A source, a spring
The fountainhead
Of life doth bring
A force of love
Enough for all who listen, who see
Not me
Nor these lines outstretched
The fountain quietly splashing in thee
Springs forth the nature of our humanity.

The Pursues Star shower

A black inky night,
Oiled the ripple licks a pebble beach.
A firmament splashes high above,
Throwing slashes of light.
Those shooting stars
Those countless shining points Illuminate.

The night
The flight
The path of unseen suns.
The orbits of planets known.
The nebula of unknown galaxies far beyond,
My sight
This night
The faint high sparkling light.
Calls & pondering,
I wonder how that ancient dust,
Once burning hot in distant star.
Now lives on in my warm blood.

Our Cells invigorate.
Our Thoughts considerate.
Our Love permeates.
The infinity of now
The eternity of how
The complexity of why.

This Summer day

When bird song floats through leaves of green
Like a butterfly so seldom seen
The sun beam sharp dissects it's might
Within the pond's clear watery light
Warmth
lies heavy in the high blue sky
An insect chirp, a babies cry
a barking dog
The quiet splash from a croaking frog
An ice cream drip, the ants they swarm
The daisy droops it's head forlorn
Nimbus clouds they threaten to storm
This calls to me
This sings to me
This speaks to me

Words in a line, call it poetry.

Today

Today I step out into the world,
My eyes shining with the joy,
I'll share with all and everything I meet.

Tonight

From me to you, a sweet goodnight through lonely hours of
Stary light
till day it dawns and with new start
You awaken, deep in my heart.

Dreams we've shared are intertwined
With memories, moments their to find
When touch & talk & laughter free,
Illuminate the the need to be,

Together, ...we share the oneness
Grown fondness, fairness all togetherness ....
A you,
An I,
In union we can touch the sky.

White, white the cold white snow

Falling petals,
from a fire the glow.
Warm the tips of
a frozen touch.

The wet driven sky,
The Leafless tree,
The pale sun gone,
The cry in me,
The crackle and split,
The words caught alight.
This winter moment,
This dark cold night.

My thoughts in flight,
Leap sparkling high.
Tossed in silver to a velvet sky.

Beyond the ice.
Beyond the snow.
Beyond golden glow.
Beyond thoughts of complex touch.

Dwell the you.
Dwell the me.
Dwell the much.
Dwell the image,
the crystal touch.

Of a morning wake.
A new born day.
Flushed your cheek
You turn my way
Whisper warm
breathing say..

I love you

Winters call

Let winters chill, grip tight the stalks & twigs of natures awe
Those crystals chip sharp leaves with white not thaw
Splendours cold throne rules all supreme,
The rest stand bare, subjugate a mood extreme.

What will push the green buds in thaw?
Spread the leaf, till abundance is once more
Let blossoms bud, roll its dainty head
Ripen bulb, fill the fruit, load the seed make the bread.

Our globe rolls on in eons spent
Again goes golden, falls, is rent
  "Now"
The Pond, hard edged with ice
A crunchy shelf skate young & old in glee
Nature sleeps, yet we adjust our sight & feel the all

Winters call
A changing mood all with procured.
A wish, a want, a simple winter day secured.

Spiritual Poems

Beyond-fullness

You are Eternity and Starlight
Dressed in the debris of creation
Tomorrow's emergent in your consciousness
Connecting it too
Loves heartbeats, the clock of limitations
Tick tock, tick tock
Flow-states of mindfulness, becoming too
Beyond
Universal and oceanic connectivity is where we
Unify and embrace this
Beyondfullness
Stillness
Oneness
Fullness

Challenge

I am challenged
I say I can't
I can I know
I go
I take the jump
I risk
I ignore the fear
I focus on the now
"It's done"
I now meet the me
I transform to anew
I grow at this edge
I know it's new
I am you
You
You too
You can go
You face fear
You say you can't

You know you can
You focus on its done
"You know"
Transformation is how we grow.

Dragonfly

When I change the perspective
From the natural to within
When I see with my inner eye, "*me and life*" unify
Magic can begin
The blade of green almost unseen thrives as mighty as the gnarled old oak
Dragonfly snaps the mite is smote
Lark song ring
Joy unfurls its wondrous wing
You
Me
Unseen
Life is a most wonderful thing
This living thriving cosmos, in which we all interweave Is one, is mine, is yours too
This universal move is new
Only after passing
Do we dissipate?
Do we untangle?

Do we disintegrate?
Live see
Alive feel
Wonder, don't be late
Open my sight, open the gate
Unificate

Emerge

Let go
Simply let your '*self*' go
Go on, do it!
For then and
Only now, you can become
Who you truly are
Who you're intrinsically meant to be
Free up
Free out
Emerge

Find Me

What ever it is that comes to me
Will go!
What ever it is that you find
Will be lost!
What ever there is that I think
Will be forgotten!
What ever it is you have done
Will be forgiven!
There
Over there across the sky, where we are all
One,
We are beyond this
To and fro
We defy description
We define a reality
Without words
Only with meanings
Come find me

Fly

To be free
To be unburdened
To be loved
Untie your wings
Loosen your feathers
Fly

God

It's not God who looks down upon you
It's not God that you gaze up to
Hanging limp from that cross
God shines forth from you
Into the eyes of those you behold
Embracing the world with wonder
This is loves thunder
This is the quiet grace
Share this joy
Step into the rich invisibility of your soul
It's echo is already waiting
Here within

Light

The body lives in the world
The mind lives in the universe
Your light though is brighter
Beautiful like sunrise
Boundless like sunset
Live in it.

Music

You, indeed you
It's late I know
But to have awoken
Is what matters
Take this gentle instrument
Into your hands
Let your fingers fly
Play, play now and forever
For the music is not yours
It's from heaven.

Peace

It’s in the peace
I hear
I feel
I see
I catch
My-Self
In communion with you.
You are this peace
You are in this place
In me too.

Searching

In all my searching, all my striving to find God
I found this, in me
In all my searching, all my striving to find Myself
I found this, in you
Funny
This moment of inflexion
Recognition
We are simply one.

Silence

Silence
is not empty
it's a universe
Which we can also inhabit
Which is a gateway to understanding
A portal to discover
Those answers
We need to find
Along our own pathway of
Development and growth
Leave the noise
Seek the silence
Find the truth
Understand the meaning
Wake up
Dancing at the spring.

Tango

When love dances
It's in the spin, in the twist
Moments in movement
Glances caught between crescendo and cantata
Magic encapsulated

My between
Your pirouette
Our tango

Its expungence and dynamic
Liquid love drips from this passion, this flow
We have become intrinsic instrumental cords
Strung between love
Harmony and more
Resonant we melt
Intimate we stamp a fragrance of eternity to this day
Perfumed in the way love moves
To Tango

The Metaphor

Find your metaphor and fill it with dance and glow
For in the orchard of your mind golden apples grow
Harvest this poetry
Rich sweet and song
Like treasured pearls
To right the wrong
To inspire the desire to move beyond
Mediocrity
Speak out with those throttled voices from inside
Crack your silence with the truth, arise
Move to your metaphor
Dancing free in space
Fill this life with love and feel the grace.

The Music

What!
Can this be true?
You still dance and laugh although
The music is yours alone
Sung in your mind
Ringing joyfully in your ears
We are never ever separated from the Divine
Even pretending ignorance is useless
We dance non the less
We laugh all the more.

The Prison

When it's the deep distant chalice
You are reaching for
Take a hammer to the dungeon wall
Grab the keys and run
Bolt as if you would be born into colour
It's urgent, it's now
For time is not the ticking off the clock
It's the writing on the wall
Remember this.

The Stream

Yonder this day, with its struggle of fear and strife
We have another life
Dancing, free and in flow
Like the stream coming from the mountain
Shed those soiled robes
Wash your sprit of that troubled self.

Who?

Who
I am not
What you think
I am
You are not
What you think
You are
You are
What you think
I am
I am
Not what I think
I am either
You are
I am too
But who are we really?

Travel Poems

Croatian night

Spread wide across the deep night sky
Sparkling star, the moon is high
Pulsing red the jetliner zooms
A wish carried quick
a shooting star dies

Dark on the beach
I close my eyes
Thoughts alight my mind it flies
To see this all
Hear the fall of a rippled wave
Touch this all with a star filled gaze

Sweet this night
A balmy breeze tickles me
Beaches me on the pebbles
It also shatters the shiny moons Reflection

Another night
Another might
Just roll over to sleep
I keep me wake
I keep my gaze
I keep my thoughts which amaze
I keep you
Yes you
who's light will roll itself around this night
Take the enchantment
take dream and in it
Be the answer to that wish

Croatian night

Holidays

Dappled sun the water blue
Sea floor strewn in radiant hew
We slowly swim with glasses tight
Mouth clenched snorkel fitting right

This Adriatic magic day
This sea, this shore, this way

The simplification
The ease
The emursion
The warmth

Holiday, hours minutes moments fade, who cares
It's now
In dappled light
Fish dressed in stripes
Dart between the rocks
Dance in silver shoals

An Octopus slinks into a crack
Here
Now
Lost in translation
Glory in my gaze.
It's now
holidays

Homo Sapien

Last night while watching a star filled night
Deep in my mind far from that light
A tear of joy a quiet yell of glee
A momentary insight shone distant in me

The Megellaniic clouds, the Milky Way and Andromeda
All far out in this galaxy filled dark
The southern Cross stars to find my mark.

The elements formed in this Milky Way
Create the helix of my DNA
Fibonacci spirals spin in the cosmic deep
Unravel too in shells we find and love to keep.

The twinkle of star light which glints the eye
Shines on thoughts the meaning of why?
We spin through life
Without the shred of an idea
How significant the coincidences are between

The Alpha and Omega
The Micro and Macrocosmic
Infinity and Eternity
The 'I Am ' and the serendipity of the universes universality

This cosmic magic is found throughout life on earth
Open minds allow the birth
The birth of a you,
new fresh, deep and true
The mystery known to non but those who ponder
Why when where
This amazing world all began.
We are Ancient

Königswinter Germany

Through this valley wide sweet & long
Vine covered slopes the Rhine flows strong
Thick the forest leaf tinged in gold
The river grips the boat it holds.
Through the folds of my open shirt
It's warm, the sky of a blue summer burnt
Wheels spin as bikes zip by
A single cloud hooks the lash on my eye
Turning in, to my thoughts profound
Solace meets the me I found
I'd lost and searched for ages long
Found last night in a dream sung song
Here I sit with a new found me
Pondering life along the Rhine Valley
My glass frosted in pearls of dew
Spätburgunder I toast the new

Miles High

Seven miles high as I flew by
You sat and watched and wondered why?
So high above
There flew a love
An answered txt an open prayer
Its happened, he fell
Right onto that chair

Onto your lap, into your life
A man a mission into your day, yes late!
But love is never to be undone
By crazy things we can't explain
By planes and games and chili hot
It's you he found
Yet she did not
Imagine how or where or why?
Could this happen
Could this man fly
Could this mean me
Could we together see

A new tomorrow's breaking bright
Loves light calling
To Carry forth and in its flight

Open new a chapter free
It's you it's who
It's me.

Shitluck Dude

He kicked the dirt with the boot heel high
Jacket dusty, jeans ripped at the thigh
Tongue cracked & dry, by nicotine & Jack D
A night at the table with cards & Mc Fee

Ace of Spades, Queen of Harts
Colours, numbers, royalty, cards
The poker made broker the longer night
Mc Fee had the hand, in the other a knife

Dude, hit the shit at a quarter to four
The cards were down, the money no more
Jack D was dry
Lucky`s gone up in smoke
He spat on the floor
No one laughed at the joke

A fist cracked his jaw
The blade sliced into his thigh

He butted Mc Fee, blood burst at the eye
Kicked in his groin, the poor bastard screamed
Game now over Lucky he seemed

Then he grabbed the bucks
Glass crashed to the floor
Notes flew through the room
Stumbled, while running out into the gloom

The tales not over, the story not done
Shitluck dude had had his fun
Then turning round with a bloodshot eye
A barrel blast and Shitluck cried !
Spun to the floor, shoulder spurting red blood
Pain was crazy as he chewed the mud
Then twisting his head
A glint still in his eye
He cracked a smile
Before he died

The Captain

Upon the bridge he took his stand
The captains look a journey planned
To distant star, it's light still dim
Blazing gold the radiant rim
Of a setting sun
against a rising tide
Moon was full the seagull cried
The urchin curled within its shell
A shooting star
to the ringing bell

Horizon cut the dark in two!

In ocean deep
We are the few to leave
the wave
the wet
the blue

Fly, through the heavens on a starry night
Sails filled with moon milky light
On sparkling spume
The firmament we'll trawl
Constellations be the ports of call
Pieces, Sagittarius, Andromeda too
To visit you wonder, the question who?

Let it be spoken
Let it be said
Those lonely souls, while you sleep in bed
Received us well
With both laughter & joy
We traded our memories, dreams, thoughts and ideas
We threw over board the worry and fears
To sunsets new rising
A waking new day
I'd passaged the cosmos
I'd found a new way

Of grabbing the moment
Of touching the pulse
Of living the fullest
Of being my most

The Club

Down at the club by the river side
The place was a buzzing
The vibe alive

Beat so sweet groove so cool I
You move toward me cross a crowded room

Oh oh ohhhh
Im on Fire on Fire

And at a glance, with a sexy stance
shrugging your shoulder
you made a pass.

Beat so sweet, groove so cool,
You move toward me cross a crowded room.

Oh oh ohhhh
Im on Fire on Fire

Electrified my heart made boom!,
Your eyes touch mine Like the big round moon.

Oh oh ohhhh
Im on Fire on Fire

Beat so sweet, groove so cool
You move towards me across a crowded room

Taking my hand, put my drink to the side
Began to dance began to glide

Beat so sweet, grove so cool
You move with me across a crowded room

Oh oh ohhhh
Im on Fire on Fire

Not a word we spoke but that intense stare
Bodies so close I could touch her hair

Beat so sweet, grove so cool
You move with me across a crowded room

Your cheek so soft, your body so lithe,
We move in rhythm,
You make a sigh.

Beat so sweet, grove so cool
You move with me across a crowded room

Oh oh ohhhh
Im on Fire on Fire

Lips they touch, it's majic pure,
Wet and moist it's love I'm sure.

Beat so sweet, grove so cool
You move with me across a crowded room

Oh oh ohhhh
Im on Fire on Fire

Body heat, we groove & jive
Feeling intense and so alive.

Beat so sweet, grove so cool
You move with me across a crowded room

Oh oh ohhhh
Im on Fire on Fire

She pushes her hips against me strong,
Feels how hard that I'm turned on.

Beat so sweet, grove so cool
You move with me across a crowded room

Oh oh ohhhh
Im on Fire on Fire

Tighter now, breasts stroke my chest,
Hands pull her buttocks,
Gives me the rest.

Beat so sweet, grove so cool
You move with me across a crowded room

Oh oh ohhhh
Im on Fire on Fire

Passion pure fills us so tight,
Oh Babe, this will be the night.

Beat so sweet, grove so cool
You move with me across a crowded room.

Oh oh ohhhh
Im on Fire on Fire

The Journey Revised

Dusty my feet
Each speck, speaks of things seen or done along life's way
Enriched with gold I say
The patina of me knocks to the opening door
Upon the floor, the dust is washed away
Remains the gold
His words invite, they hold
Me shining, for this new day
A journeys end I'm whole
My home, my soul, my way

The Leaving

Leaving, we kiss & say goodbye.
Our cheeks they touch,
The sparkle in your eye I love so much.

Gone.
Gone again.
Gone the days of simple fun,
The moments of laughter, talking, one on one.

Now your perfumed scent,
The warmth meant meaning of this love.
The love we know is right & strong.

Or is it right & still is wrong?

Gone
Gone again
Gone alone we ask & find a lonely answer in the pain.

Why, a question?
My cheeks now dry.
To wait, until again we touch & laugh & sigh.
Wonder in our thoughts,
The memories of a ribbon in your hair,
How I stumbled on the stair.

Gone
Gone again
Gone as if in air, I ask again is this really fair?

The glance thrown across your shoulder, blade.
The stance, hips twisted tight upon steel stilettos.
The attitude, flux exhaling in warm summer air.

Leaving, we kiss & say goodbye.
Our cheeks they touch,
The sparkle you leave in me,
I love so much.

The Malvern Hills

Green & fair is England's land
The fields fair hue in green & tan
Rows, hedges, Trees are grand
Hilled the Malvern since time began

The Spring of St. Ann
Splashes clean & fresh
From a font in marble clad
Where lords & ladies, the gentry who
Came & drank this healthy brew

From here....
A steep track winds both too and fro
The beacon hidden, I'm far below
But take me there this way will go
To a morning view with the World below

Awakening, plumed in veils of grey
The golden orbs light lifting day
Is England's green with morning crowned
This Jerusalem shines, is so profound

The Muse

Morning, harbour bathed in glow
Boats bob, the ripples flow, reflecting gold
Behind me clouds dark fill the sky
My journey starts, a tear wet eye
Richness all around to see
Day born moment wakes in me
Bag clatter echoes from the cobbled stone
Seagulls screeching heard alone
Jellyfish pulse in the cold wet blue
A whispered word deep in my ear
My muse awakes with a laugh clear call
Reach out touch embrace this ALL
Then smile and set it free once more

The Prehistoric Artist

A million years of renting crack
The ripping grind of broken rock
Continental plates in
motion
broke this massive
This mighty mountain ranges back

The Cederberg of Africa threw
this rock anew
the ledges
the caves
the wind eroded throws of stone
Here made ancient man, his hunting home

Those tribes of San, of Koi, of Bushman old
Emerged in nature's abundant realm
Where beasts, the lion and giraffe did roam
With men, women the children too

Skilled they knew the crafts of life
The skill of nature's natural path
Hunter finder gatherer singer story teller & painter who
Marked the stone with a colored hue

Figures in groups
Hunters alone
Women carrying children home.
They marked their hands as gift or proof
They painted antelope on a sloping roof
These are the artists of ancient lore.
The shaman the magic the seers of all.
The witness of men long long before

Now!

Genius deep in a creative mind
Made an image of the life he found
On the hunt
On the hill
In the valley below
In the stream stoney falls
Between crags & scrub
His creatures now dance on stoney rough
Floating he paints with a feather brush
His mind free and far far away
This magic moment of infinity finds
The eternity of this great-full day

The artist
the creative mind of man
till this day

Today

Thoughts on an Ice-cream

Should love taste sweet, Like the ice cream in my hand
It's flavours of stracciatella, vanilla and double chocolate
Linger on my tongue but cold
Still the sun illuminates
Warms the heart in me
Melting my awe leaving me the delicious taste of love
All is flow, hot with cold
Here and there, you and me
Move through my senses, out to the horizon
Back to my book, onto my taste buds

Am I tasting our connectivity?
Or is this refreshing moment inducing you?
Am I being seduced by life itself?

What joy
What harmony
What simple peace
I find

Floundering in my head
Laughing quietly instead
Of wiping away those troubled sticky drops.
Fallen sweetly to my daily bread

Traveller

When you are away away
Gone off travelling on the planes
I'm fine with you, believe me
I'm still connected to your soul
The window in your heart is open too
Through which I fly
when the lights go down
Also then when a cloud passes above my memories
Rain patters softly on my place of quiet rectitude
It's fond sweet wine, those memories
Each wrapped in crinkly lilac foil
Dissolve on my tongue
With the morning cry of seagulls
Echoing through the open curtains
You return.

When will you Return

From me to you, a sweet goodnight
Then lonely hours of starry light
Till day it dawns and with new start
Again you awaken, in my heart

Dreams we've shared are intertwined
With memories, moments their to find
When touch & talk & laughter free
Illuminate the need to be

Together
We share the oneness
Grown fondness, fairness all togetherness

A union, we kiss and laugh and cry
As if time had never touched us two
It's me
It's you
It's who we have always been and done.

Before and even now
I'll wait
Prepare a cup of tea
Soon, soon again.
It's you
who will return, here to me

Who you are!!!

As the days they come & go
It is as if Ive always known
That out there & far away
Beyond my sight,
Beyond the flight,
Of thought, of touch & feel,
The person you so real,
Lives floating on a cloud.
Of colours bright & gay,
Of sounds & song away
Away, I calling say
Listen to the cheep
Listen to the creeping,
Hands of moments lost,
Of minutes found.
Of feelings, memories so profound
They might just, adjust anew the times
I've had & shared with you.
The thoughts are yours,

From mine they intertwine,
Create anew an image,
My memory of who,
You are.
What we have become,
Where we still have to go & do.
Am I the fool ...???
just laughing cause of who.....
I am to you.

Printed in Germany
by Amazon Distribution
GmbH, Leipzig

19020485R00136